Nevada Public Library

631 K Avenue

Nevada, Iowa 50201

515-382-2628

DEMCO

Children
of the
RELOCATION
CAMPS

Children
of the
RELOCATION
CAMPS

Catherine A. Welch

PICTURE
the
AMERICAN
PAST

Carolrhoda Books, Inc./Minneapolis

To the memory of my grandparents, Italian immigrants

Front cover: Children at an assembly center wave American flags.
Back cover: Two boys at an assembly center in May 1942
Page one: In Los Angeles, California, Yoichi and Senichi Sumi wait for the train that will take them to Manzanar Relocation Center.
Page two: The Mochida family awaits relocation.
Page five: Children sing "White Christmas" during a Christmas program at Heart Mountain Relocation Center in Wyoming in 1943.

Carolrhoda Books, Inc.
A Division of Lerner Publishing Group
241 First Avenue North
Minneapolis, MN 55401 U.S.A.

Website address: www.lernerbooks.com

LIBRARY OF CONGRESS CATALOGING-IN-PUBLICATION DATA

Welch, Catherine A.
   Children of the relocation camps / Catherine A. Welch.
     p. cm. — (Picture the American past)
   Includes bibliographical references and index.
   Summary: Explores the experiences of Japanese American children who were moved with their families to relocation centers during World War II, looking at school, meals, sports, and other aspects of camp life.
   ISBN 1-57505-350-0
   1. World War, 1939–1945—Children—United States—Juvenile literature. 2. World War, 1939–1945—Concentration camps—United States—Juvenile literature. 3. Japanese Americans—Evacuation and relocation, 1942–1945—Juvenile literature. [1. Japanese Americans—Evacuation and relocation, 1942–1945. 2.World War, 1939–1945—Children. 3. World War, 1939–1945—Concentration camps.] I. Title. II. Series.
D769.8.A6 W45 2000
940.53'161—dc21   99-006860

Manufactured in the United States of America
1 2 3 4 5 6 – JR – 05 04 03 02 01 00

CONTENTS

Above: Ships burn during the Japanese attack on Pearl Harbor.
Opposite page: Japanese Americans in San Francisco await relocation.

LEAVING HOME BEHIND

*Why us? I felt like we were just
being punished for nothing.*
—Emi Somekawa, who was sent
to Tule Lake Relocation Center

The Japanese are bombing Pearl Harbor!" Radio voices cried out the news. Japanese warplanes had attacked a United States naval base in Hawaii.

It was December 7, 1941. Americans were stunned. More than two thousand people were killed. The next day, President Franklin Roosevelt declared war on Japan. The United States entered World War II, which had begun in Europe in 1939.

Japanese American children say the Pledge of Allegiance with their classmates in San Francisco in early 1942.

At that time, about 120,000 Japanese Americans lived on the West Coast. Many lived near airports and navy shipyards. Some other Americans feared they would destroy those places. They feared Japanese Americans would spy on them and send information to Japan.

In truth, Japanese Americans were loyal to the United States. They had chosen it as their home, and they lived like other Americans. Families worked and attended church. Children went to school and played with friends.

Hours after the attack on Pearl Harbor, government agents knocked on the doors of Japanese American homes. The agents searched houses for signs of loyalty to Japan. Some children watched agents take their fathers away to prison, even though their fathers had not committed a crime.

A government agent searches a Japanese American home.

Families were afraid to keep treasured objects brought from Japan. Children watched their parents bury Japanese books and swords. Seven-year-old Jeanne Wakatsuki saw her father burn a Japanese flag. "I couldn't believe he was doing that," she said.

Two weeks later, government agents took him away. He was a fisher. They were afraid that he would help enemy Japanese ships.

The Japanese American owner of this store put up a sign to remind his neighbors that he was an American citizen. The store was later closed.

Some Americans used signs like this one to express their feelings about Japanese Americans.

Soon children saw signs on store windows. They said things like "No Japs Allowed." Angry voices on the radio said, "Send the Japs back to Japan!" Japanese American children were afraid to go to school. Some white children would not eat lunch with them. Others called them nasty names.

One girl asked twelve-year-old Joanne Ono, "Why did you bomb Pearl Harbor?"

In February of 1942, the government issued Executive Order 9066. It said that Japanese Americans in western states could be evacuated, or forced to leave their homes. Over the next few months, people learned when they had to leave. They would be moved to camps called assembly centers. Meanwhile, the government began building ten permanent relocation centers.

Japanese Americans did not understand. The country was also at war with Germany and Italy. Why weren't Germans and Italians being sent away?

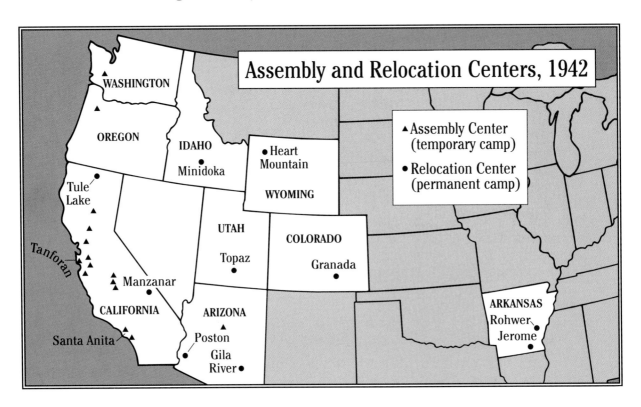

This boy searches for his family's name on a poster. Posters showed families which bus would take them to an assembly center.

Once a family received their orders, they had about a week to pack. Each person could bring two bags. Eleven-year-old Ben Takeshita remembered, "We were told by our parents to wear as much as we could . . . several shirts and jackets."

Adults had to sell their homes, stores, and furniture. Most received little or no money.

No one was allowed to bring pets. Children hugged dogs and cats good-bye and watched strangers take them away.

A young girl waits for a bus with her family's bags.

Each family was given a number. The day they left, parents put identification tags on suitcases and on children's coats.

Some neighbors brought the children gifts and wished them luck. But some did not. Many people were afraid of being called "Jap lovers."

On the day they were relocated, this family huddled together, and the children held on to favorite toys.

Japanese Americans board a train in Seattle, Washington, in April 1942. Friends and relatives wave good-bye from a bridge.

Families reported to churches and railroad stations. They waited for buses or trains. Soldiers with guns kept everyone moving.

A soldier checks a young boy's identification tag.

Children tried to be brave. Twelve-year-old Donald Nakahata said, "I had this fear of being left behind." No one knew what the future held. They only knew that they had lost their homes and their freedom.

Above: The Santa Anita Assembly Center was built on a racetrack. The parking lot became the site of hundreds of temporary homes known as barracks.
Opposite page: Military police stand guard in a watchtower at Santa Anita.

Life in the Camps

This is what we did with our days.
We loved and we lived just like people.
—Mitsuye Yamada, who was sent to
Minidoka Relocation Center at age 19

The first camps were temporary assembly centers. The U.S. government built them on racetracks and fairgrounds. A barbed-wire fence surrounded each camp. Soldiers with guns watched from towers. The people in the camps were prisoners—they could not leave.

For many people, horse stalls were their new homes. The stalls were small, dusty, and smelly. Spider webs stuck to the whitewashed walls.

Children moved their few things into empty rooms. One light bulb hung from the ceiling. There was no running water. The bathrooms were worse. They were in another building, in one big room. There was no privacy.

Tanforan Assembly Center. Five people lived in the two small rooms of this family apartment, which had once been a horse stall.

For meals, children stood in line with tin plates and cups. The white cooks did not understand Japanese ways. Japanese people did not eat rice with sweet food. But some cooks served them canned apricots poured over rice.

Families stood in line for meals in large buildings called mess halls.

After a few months, the permanent relocation centers were finished. Families had to pack up and move again. Two camps were on swampland in Arkansas. Most were in remote desert areas, far from cities and highways.

Twelve-year-old Emiko Sasaki said, "The first few days in Topaz [Relocation Center], I walked about carefully, for I had heard that coyotes and poison scorpions were about."

Like most of the camps, Heart Mountain Relocation Center was built on dry, dusty land owned by the government.

Manzanar. Children run for cover during a dust storm.

At some camps, there were dust storms. The sky grew dark. The wind howled. Everyone rushed inside. When it was over, children were left with the taste of dust in their mouths.

A father shelters his sons from the rain with a Japanese parasol.

Then came rain. Kazue Tsuchiyama said, "The mud sticks like paste on shoes and boots while the people slip about in the soft deep mud."

At first, most rooms did not have heat. Children shivered in the cold mornings. "Your body is shaking just like a skeleton when you are putting on your clothes," said Dorothy Obato.

The barracks were poorly built and cheerless. Everyone tried hard to make them feel like home. People put pictures on the walls and hung curtains. Some made chairs and tables from scraps of wood.

Tule Lake. Homemade furniture and shelves decorate this family's apartment.

Rohwer. Students attend class in an empty barracks.

Most Japanese Americans tried to make the best of camp life. Schools were started in empty buildings. At first, classrooms had no chairs, blackboards, or heat stoves. "Some students brought cans of charcoal to school and warmed themselves," said Sumiko Ikeda. Sometimes several students had to share one book.

In school, children said the Pledge of Allegiance. They sang songs like "God Bless America." For Thanksgiving, they made craft projects of cardboard cabins and Pilgrims.

A boy models for an art class. Signs on the walls encourage students to help with the United States' efforts to win the war.

Granada. Boys tend a garden near their barracks school.

People planted victory gardens and grew their own food. The soil was usually dry or muddy. But families bought seeds from catalogs and planted vegetables. Children helped carry buckets of water to the gardens. Some families were able to raise livestock. Children fed pigs, chickens, and ducks.

Many people tried to bring beauty into the camps. They collected cactuses and other plants. They built Japanese-style stone gardens.

The gardens brought some joy, but they did not bring freedom. Children were warned not to play close to the barbed wire. Ben Takeshita said, "Topaz felt like a prison. . . . One older man . . . went too close to the fence, and the guards shot him."

Manzanar. This man built a garden of stones along his barracks home.

Children make artificial flowers at the Manzanar Art School.

People found many ways to pass the time. Every camp offered classes in *ikebana*, the Japanese art of flower arranging. Children made flowers and leaves from newspaper, cloth, and other scraps.

Children joined the Boy Scouts, Girl Scouts, and singing clubs. They watched Abbott and Costello movies and made kites to fly. On holidays, they staged plays for their parents.

But they did not forget their old friends. "We wonder if our friends back home still miss us," said Sumiko Ikeda.

Heart Mountain. Girl Scouts march in a holiday parade.

Children found moments of fun and laughter playing basketball, football, and baseball. Baseball was the favorite sport. At Manzanar Relocation Center, eighty baseball teams were formed.

Manzanar. Sixth graders enjoy a game of softball. A rock serves as home plate.

Christmas Eve, 1943, at Granada Relocation Center. Children decorate a donated Christmas tree with paper trimmings.

Older children tried hard to make Christmas a happy event for younger children. "We thought that no one would think of us," said Emiko Kamiyo. So they planned a party and decorated the mess hall.

Japanese Americans did their best to stay hopeful. But they were eager to be free.

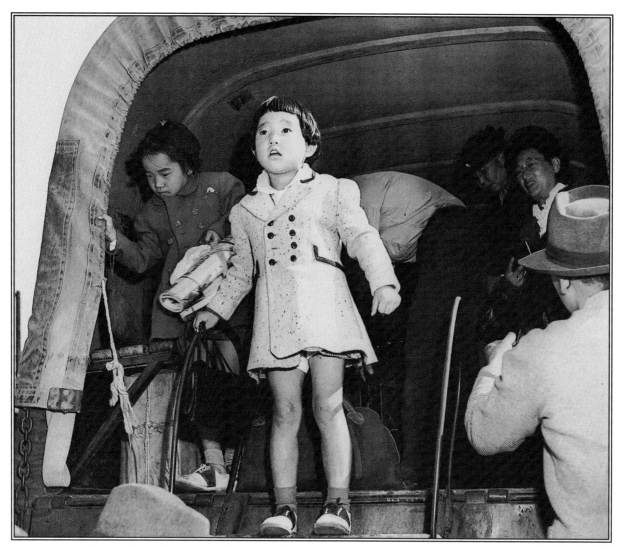

Above: Two girls arrive at the Granada train station on their way home to California. Opposite page: A grave at Granada Relocation Center. During the time the camp was open, 107 people died there.

Starting Over

Sometimes you day-dream in class. . . .
Will it be the same when you return?
—Dorothy Obato, who was sent to Poston
Relocation Center while in high school

On December 18, 1944, the U.S. Supreme Court said that keeping loyal citizens in relocation camps was unlawful. By 1945, World War II was coming to an end. During that year, the government began to close the camps and allow Japanese Americans to leave.

Children were excited. But they were also scared. Where would they live? How would their classmates treat them?

The Tanioka and Kuniyoshi families returned to their farms in Merced, California, in June 1945.

Japanese Americans had to find new jobs and new places to live. Many families moved to the East Coast. A few moved to Japan. Some people returned to their homes in western states.

Most had lost their farms or businesses. A few had neighbors who had cared for their property. But many people found their things destroyed or stolen.

Families who had stored their belongings in this building in Los Angeles, California, returned to find them destroyed.

Poston. The Hirano family holds a portrait of their son and brother, who served in the U.S. Army during World War II.

Families welcomed home sons and brothers who had fought in the war. Many Japanese American men had joined the army and fought bravely. They wanted to show their loyalty to the United States. Many had been wounded. Some lost their lives.

Families started over. Children went to new schools or returned to their old ones.

Many Japanese Americans wanted to forget the relocation camps. But others wanted people to remember their stories. They never wanted anything like this to happen again—to any group of people.

The site of the Manzanar camp was made a National Historic Site in 1992.

CREATING BEAUTY

Making a Japanese Stone Garden

Japanese people who came to live in the United States brought many traditions with them. Even during the hard times of the relocation camps, Japanese Americans continued to practice these traditions. One was *ikebana*, the art of flower arranging, shown on page 30.

Another tradition was the Japanese art of dry landscape gardens, known as *karesansui*. The gardens are used as places to pray, think, and rest. Adults and children in the relocation camps found peace and comfort in creating these beautiful gardens.

Water, stones, and plants are used in many types of Japanese gardens. For *karensansui*, real water is not used. Instead, gravel, pebbles, or sand are used to symbolize, or stand for, water. Stones symbolize natural objects, such as mountains, islands, and boats in the sea. In modern *karesansui*, moss and other plants are also used.

Here's how you can make your own Japanese stone garden.

Japanese Stone Garden

a box about the size of a shirt box (about 15″ x 9 1/2″ x 2 1/2″)
enough sand or pebbles to fill the box up to 1/2 inch from the top
two stones of different sizes
one smaller stone
one somewhat flat stone
a small rake, or wide-toothed comb
moss or other small plants

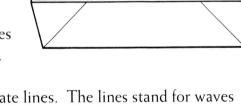

1. Choose stones that are not too big or too small for your box. Stones should be a dark color, such as black, brown, or gray.

2. Fill the box with sand or pebbles to about 1/2 inch from the top.

3. Rake the sand or pebbles to create lines. The lines stand for waves in a sea.

4. At one end of the box, arrange the two largest stones. They stand for mountains. Add the flat stone. It stands for an island.

5. Sink the stones into the sand or pebbles. About two-thirds of each stone should be buried.

6. Sink the smallest stone near the other end of the box. It stands for a boat.

7. Rake a circular pattern to create ripples around the mountain and island stones. Add moss or small plants near the mountain stones.

8. Enjoy your Japanese stone garden. Try making other gardens by placing different stones in a new way.

NOTE TO TEACHERS AND ADULTS

For children, the days of the relocation camps may seem like part of a distant and far-off past. But there are many ways to make this event and its people come alive. Along with helping children create a Japanese stone garden, you can explore the Japanese American relocation camps of America's past in other ways. One way is to read more about the camps. More books on the topic are listed on pages 45 and 46. Another way to explore the past is to train young readers to study historical photographs. Historical photographs hold many clues about how life was lived in earlier times.

Ask your children or students to look for the details and "read" all the information in each picture in this book. For example, why do the barracks shown in the photos on pages 18, 22, 23, and 31 look the same? (To build the camps quickly and inexpensively, the government used the same design and materials over and over.) To encourage young readers to learn to read historical photographs, have them try these activities:

Packing Up and Leaving Home

Study the photos on pages 14 to 17 of the evacuation and relocation of 1942. Based on what you can see and what you have read, write a list of all the things a Japanese American child might have packed to take to a relocation camp. Remember that each person was allowed to bring only two bags or suitcases. Next, imagine that you are being moved to a place similar to a relocation camp. Write a list of the things you would take with you. Compare your lists. How is your personal list different from the first list? How would your list change if you could only bring two suitcases? What things would you leave behind?

Keeping a Journal

Many Japanese Americans kept written records of their lives during the time of the relocation camps. Imagine yourself as a young Japanese American living on the West Coast in the early 1940s. Describe what it was like for you on the days following the Japanese attack on Pearl Harbor. How did your classmates treat you? Write about the day you learned that your family was being evacuated. How did you and your family react? What did you do to prepare? Next, describe your arrival at an assembly center and what it was like there. Then write about moving to a permanent relocation center. What was your family's room like? What did you do to make it feel more like home? Include entries about school and playing with friends. For more details about the times of the relocation camps, read *The Bracelet*, *The Children of Topaz*, and *Journey to Topaz*.

Having Fun

Make a list of your favorite things to do for fun. Include places away from home where you go to have fun. Also include any objects that you use to have fun, such as sports equipment, toys, or video games. Next, imagine that you have been evacuated to a relocation camp. Go back to your list and cross off the things you can no longer do. Also cross off the objects that you could not bring to a camp. How has your list changed? Study the photographs on pages 24 to 33 of children's activities in the camps. Can you think of new things to do for fun in a camp? See if you can add more items to your list, using only what you could have brought in two suitcases. To learn more about how children had fun in the relocation camps, read *Baseball Saved Us* and *The Children of Topaz*.

RESOURCES ON THE RELOCATION CAMPS

Bunting, Eve. *So Far from the Sea.* Illustrated by Chris K. Soentpiet. New York: Clarion Books, 1998. In this picture book for young readers, seven-year-old Laura and her family visit the site of Manzanar Relocation Center in 1972. Laura's father shares his memories of living in the camp.

Hamanaka, Sheila. *The Journey: Japanese Americans, Racism, and Renewal.* New York: Orchard Books, 1990. Using text and closeup photographs of details from a large mural, author Hamanaka depicts the history of Japanese people in America. The mural, painted by the author, is shown in full at the end of the book.

Houston, Jeanne Wakatsuki, and James D. Houston. *Farewell to Manzanar.* Boston: Houghton Mifflin, 1973. In this book for older readers, Jeanne Wakatsuki Houston tells the true story of her day-to-day life during the three and a half years she lived in Manzanar Relocation Center.

Mochizuki, Ken. *Baseball Saved Us.* Illustrated by Dom Lee. Lee & Low Books Inc., 1993. With text and pictures, this picture book describes how "Shorty," a young boy in a relocation camp, helps his father build a baseball field and becomes a better player.

Stanley, Jerry. *I Am an American: A True Story of Japanese Internment.* New York: Crown Publishers, Inc., 1994. Author Stanley tells the story of the Japanese American experience during World War II. This photo-essay focuses especially on the life of Shi Nomura, a high-school boy at the time.

Tunnell, Michael O., and George W. Chilcoat. *The Children of Topaz: The Story of a Japanese-American Internment Camp: Based on a Classroom Diary.* New York: Holiday House, 1996. Through photographs, text, and the daily diary of a third-grade class, this book describes life at Topaz Relocation Center.

Uchida, Yoshiko. *The Bracelet.* Illustrated by Joanna Yardley. New York: Philomel Books, 1993. Based on the author's own experiences, this picture book tells the story of seven-year-old Emi, who must leave her best friend behind when her family is relocated.

Uchida, Yoshiko. *Journey to Topaz: A Story of the Japanese-American Evacuation.* Illustrated by Donald Carrick. Berkeley, Cal.: Creative Arts Book Company, 1985. This fictional story for middle readers shares one girl's story of evacuation, relocation, and life at Topaz Relocation Center.

Yancey, Diane. *Life in a Japanese American Internment Camp.* San Diego, Cal.: Lucent Books, 1998. This book for older readers discusses events leading up to the relocation, life in the camps, and what happened after the camps were closed.

New Words

assembly center: a temporary camp for Japanese Americans who were forced to leave their homes in 1942

barracks: a building similar to a shed or barn that is used as a home for many people

evacuate: to force someone to move from home to another place

ikebana: the Japanese art of flower arranging

karesansui: the Japanese art of creating dry landscape gardens

relocation center: a permanent camp built to house Japanese Americans who had been forced to leave their homes in 1942

victory garden: a home garden planted by Americans during World War II, to allow farmers to send more farm crops to American soldiers

Index

TIME LINE

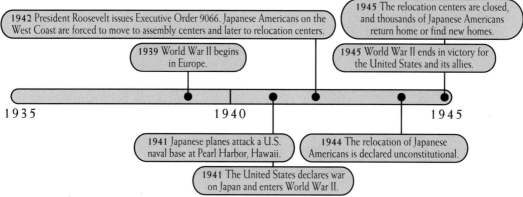

1935   1940   1945

1942 President Roosevelt issues Executive Order 9066. Japanese Americans on the West Coast are forced to move to assembly centers and later to relocation centers.

1945 The relocation centers are closed, and thousands of Japanese Americans return home or find new homes.

1939 World War II begins in Europe.

1945 World War II ends in victory for the United States and its allies.

1941 Japanese planes attack a U.S. naval base at Pearl Harbor, Hawaii.

1944 The relocation of Japanese Americans is declared unconstitutional.

1941 The United States declares war on Japan and enters World War II.

ABOUT THE AUTHOR

Catherine A. Welch lives in Monroe, Connecticut, with her husband and two children. She is the author of several books for children published by Carolrhoda, including *Clouds of Terror, Danger at the Breaker, Margaret Bourke-White: Racing with a Dream,* and *Ida B. Wells-Barnett: Powerhouse with a Pen.* She grew up in New York City and says, "I don't remember learning much in school about the Japanese Americans who were forced into camps—I'm not sure it was even mentioned. I hope young readers today will learn about the stories of the Japanese Americans who lived through this major event of World War II. Their stories show vividly how fear and prejudice can drive a country to make a mistake with terrible consequences."

ACKNOWLEDGMENTS

The author thanks the following people, who helped in gathering material for this book: Ingrid Davis, Liane Zane, and staff of Monroe (Connecticut) Public Library; Kara Paw-Pa, National Japanese American Historical Society, San Francisco; Sharon Perry, University Library, California State University, Fullerton; Kathleen R. Frazee, Oral History Program at California State University, Fullerton; Roberta Medford, University Research Library, University of California, Los Angeles. The publisher gratefully acknowledges the use of quotations from the following sources: Edwin Hiroto, ed., *Through Innocent Eyes.* Los Angeles: Keiro Services, 1990; From *Farewell to Manzanar* by James D. and Jeanne Wakatsuki Houston. Copyright © 1973 by James D. Houston. Reprinted by permission of Houghton Mifflin Company. All rights reserved; Frank and Joanne Iritani, *Ten Visits.* San Mateo, Calif.: Japanese American Curriculum Project, Inc., 1994; Emiko Sasaki, "I Was Re-located," *Senior Scholastic,* New York: Scholastic, 5/19/47; John Tateishi, *And Justice for All (An Oral History of the Japanese American Detention Camps)* Seattle: Univ. of Washington Press, 1999; Mitsuye Yamada, "The Watchtower," *Camp Notes and Other Poems.* © 1992 by Mitsuye Yamada—reprinted by permission of the author and of Kitchen Table: Women of Color Press, PO Box 40-4920, Brooklyn, NY 11240-4920. The photographs in this book are reproduced through the courtesy of: UPI/Corbis-Bettmann, front cover, pp. 11, 15, 16, 18, 21; The National Archives, back cover (210-G-3C-310), pp. 7 (210-G-2-C423), 8 (NWDNS-210-G-A78), 10 (RG-210-G-2A-35), 13 (NWDNS-210-G-C213), 14 (234), 17 (210-G-2-C417), 19 (NWDNS-210-G-B388), 20 (210-G-3C-594), 22 (RG-210-G-8E61), 23 (156), 24 (NWDNS-210-G-B428), 25 (NWDNS-210-G-D257), 26 (NWDNS-210-G-E382), 27 (RG-210-G-A-760), 28 (NWDNS-210-G-E875), 29 (NWDNS-210-G-C865), 30 (NWDNS-210-G-C901), 32 (NWDNS-210-G-A925), 33 (NWDNS-210-G-G245), 34 (NWDNS-210-G-K385), 35 (NWDNS-210-G-K410), 36 (NWDNS-210-G-14-R-1), 37 (WRA Collection), 38 (210-CC-S-26C); The Library of Congress, pp. 1 (LC-USF-3301-13289M5), 5 (LC-USZ62-12513), 6 (LC-USW33-38539), 31 (LC-USZ62-10643), 39 (LC-A351-3-M-28); Corbis-Bettmann, p. 2; AP/Wide World Photos, p. 9.